WHAT EVERY TEACHER NEEDS TO KNOW ABOUT

Curriculum

Developed by the
Christian Education Staff
of The General Board of Discipleship
of The United Methodist Church

DISCIPLESHIP RESOURCES

P.O. BOX 340003 • NASHVILLE, TN 37203-0003
www.discipleshipresources.org

This booklet was developed by the Christian Education Staff of the General Board of Discipleship of The United Methodist Church. It is one in a series of booklets designed to provide essential knowledge for teachers. Members of the staff who helped write and develop this series are Terry Carty, Bill Crenshaw, Donna Gaither, Rick Gentzler, Mary Alice Gran, Susan Hay, Betsey Heavner, Diana Hynson, Carol Krau, MaryJane Pierce Norton, Deb Smith, Julia Wallace, and Linda Whited.

Reprinted 2002, 2003

Cover and book design by Joey McNair
Cover illustration by Mike Drake

Edited by Debra D. Smith and Cindy S. Harris

ISBN 0-88177-368-9

DR368

Contents

This booklet is dedicated to
YOU,
a teacher of
children, youth, or adults,
WHO,
with fear, excitement, joy,
and commitment,
allows God *to lead you*
in the call to
TEACH.

The gifts he gave were that some would be . . .
teachers, . . . for building up the body of Christ.
(Ephesians 4:11-12)

Introduction

In accepting the invitation to teach in your congregation, you have entered into a time of growing as a Christian while you lead others in growing along with you. Whether you are a teacher of children, youth, or adults, curriculum selection and use is important to your teaching. Numerous religious and denominational bookstores with shelves full of printed curriculum pieces are available to you. Choosing just the right curriculum for a church school class can be a daunting experience.

This booklet is designed to provide you with basic knowledge of what curriculum is and how to use curriculum effectively. Depending on your previous background and experience, this booklet may serve as a crash course in the basics of curriculum selection and use, or as an encouragement to broaden your current understanding of curriculum and to consider some new possibilities.

Teachers and small-group leaders are always growing in faith. As teachers we pay attention to our relationships with God and with others. We seek to live our faith in our daily lives. We seek to find helpful resources for people to seek God, respond to God's grace, and find support and encouragement for living as disciples in the world.

This booklet is one of ten that will equip you for teaching. Use the entire series to reinforce your own knowledge, skills, and abilities.

Other booklets in this series are

What Every Teacher Needs to Know About

- *the Bible*
- *Christian Heritage*
- *Classroom Environment*
- *Faith Language*
- *Living the Faith*
- *People*
- *Teaching*
- *Theology*
- *The United Methodist Church*

Tending the Soul

I enjoy gardening. Come February, when it is still cold outside and the seed catalogs begin arriving, I begin planning how my garden will look in the upcoming growing season. Over the years gardening has become easier for me as I have discovered the tools and equipment to properly deal with the task at hand. Using a rake to weed my garden when a hoe is what I really need makes the chore laborious and time-consuming. By taking the time to assess the situation, I can make a much better selection of the type of tool I need to use. The tools I use in my garden make my work easier, not harder.

Teaching is much like tending a garden. We prepare the soil, plant seeds, fertilize, and water in preparation for the harvest. All of this can be made easier by the tools we use for the task at hand.

Teaching, as with gardening, involves asking the question, What do I need to know? Or perhaps, more appropriate for a class situation, What do *we* need to know? What is it that we need to know in order to continue growing in the Christian faith? How do we learn about it? What will the end results be after our time together is over?

As Christians we are on a lifetime journey of discovering who we are as children of God. As we travel on this journey, we need to develop skills that will help us live faithfully in our everyday settings. We need places and settings to reflect upon the Christian story so that we can incorporate its truths into our lives. We need to be a part of a nurturing community that will sustain us. As we ask questions about how we do these things, we are beginning to raise questions and concerns about curriculum.

For Personal Reflection

What are the tools you currently use as you teach? When you hear the word *curriculum*, what images come to your mind?

What Is Curriculum?

When you think of curriculum, what images come to mind? Do you see a map, something that helps you get from point A to point B? Maybe you see a recipe, with all the right ingredients for a delicious cake. Or perhaps you see a smorgasbord, which gives you a variety of choices.

Many times when we think of curriculum the only image that comes to mind is study books filled with facts and information. If someone were to ask us what we are studying in our class, we would probably answer with the name of the printed materials we are using rather than saying that we are studying what it means to be a United Methodist Christian in today's world.

One definition of *curriculum* is the planned interaction of class members with the content of the faith, materials, resources, and one another. Another definition of *curriculum* is what we teach, study, and learn in the community of faith. Curriculum includes what we teach and how we teach it.

Curriculum is more than acquiring facts and information about a certain topic, subject, or situation. Curriculum assists in the transformation of our lives. For instance, Bible study is important in the life of a Christian. The Bible helps us understand God, God's love, the ministry of Jesus, and many other important things. But if we read the Bible only for the *information* it has to offer, we may miss its power to *form* our attitudes, our values, and our lives.

It has been said that the church teaches in everything that it does. If we accept this idea, then every thing and every person in the church is part of the curriculum of the Christian faith.

Printed Curriculum Resources

Printed curriculum resources are usually the first thing given to you when you agree to teach.

Printed resources are the printed curriculum materials that have been developed to enhance effective teaching and to help guide us in studying and learning. They are those materials that furnish the content of what we will be studying and teaching in a class setting, along with many suggestions for teaching the lessons and content. They are tools that help us study and learn what we need to know.

Most printed curriculum for Sunday school either begins with the Bible and helps class members apply the teaching of the Bible to daily life, or begins with life issues that class members are facing and looks to the Bible for help in dealing with these issues. The first approach is called Bible-to-life; the second is called life-to-Bible.

The curriculum resources you use are part of an overall educational plan that usually encompasses a particular number of years. For example, some children's curriculum resources are designed to cover major themes of the Bible over a three-year or four-year cycle. Many churches use curriculum resources that are based on the Uniform Series International Bible Lessons for Christian Teaching, frequently referred to as the Uniform Series. In this ecumenical plan, weekly Scriptures and themes are selected that cover the Bible over a six-year period. Religious publishers then develop curriculum resources based on this plan.

Curriculum resources are usually printed with a specific age level in mind. You will find printed curriculum created specifically for preschool, kindergarten, younger elementary, older elementary, junior high, senior high, young adult, adult, and older adult age levels.

Dated Curriculum Resources

Dated curriculum materials usually have a specific date printed somewhere on the page. They are intended to be used on a certain date and are usually available for purchase for a limited time. Dated curriculum generally comes quarterly. The content is divided into units of study. The content of each unit is divided into a preset number of sessions and comes with suggested conversation, questions, and activities.

Dated curriculum often follows the seasons of the church year: Advent, Christmas, Season After the Epiphany, Lent, Easter, and Season After Pentecost. Some other dated curriculum is based on the lectionary. A lectionary is a set of Scripture readings for each Sunday of the year. It includes lessons from the Old Testament; the Psalms; the Gospels (Matthew, Mark, Luke, and John); and the rest of the New Testament. Many clergy use the lectionary to select the Scripture to be used in worship.

Undated Curriculum Resources

Undated curriculum materials can be used at almost any time. They are planned for use over a period ranging from a few weeks to several months, depending on the topic. Undated curriculum is available for purchase over an extended time period. Most undated curriculum deals with specific topics, such as Christian parenting, the book of John, or United Methodist heritage.

Sometimes these materials are designed in such a way that they can be used more than once. For example, some churches store used, undated curriculum in a "curriculum closet" so that it can be used again by another group in the future.

Some books that are designed primarily for individual reading also have a study guide in the back of the book or as a separate piece. When used in a group setting, these books become an undated curriculum resource.

Curriculum Components

Curriculum resources often include a variety of components, such as a teacher book, a student book, leaflets that are sent home with students, cassette tapes or compact disks, videos, and so forth. Often there will be a resource packet that includes posters, pictures, maps, and other learning aides.

Some resources include a book or packet of reproducible pages. You will need to make copies of such pages before class. (Note: You should make copies only of material that is specifically designated as reproducible. It is not appropriate to make copies of curriculum resources to avoid purchasing them.)

When you receive your curriculum, you will want to check and see that you have all of the components that you will need. It can be frustrating to plan to do a learning activity and then discover that you don't have the component needed to do it.

The Teacher's Guide

One of the first things a teacher needs to do upon receiving printed curriculum is determine where the teacher helps are located. Sometimes teacher helps can be found at the beginning of a lesson or in the back of the printed curriculum.

Often there is a separate teacher book that accompanies the curriculum. This book usually contains an overview for the unit of study, helps about the age level being taught, and teaching plans for each lesson. It also explains how to use the student book, activity packet, charts, and other curriculum components.

Beyond the Printed Resources

Curriculum resources are not just printed resources. A wide variety of materials and methods can become part of your curriculum.

Think of the variety of music available to you. Hymns, contemporary Christian music, and secular music can all help the class come alive.

If you are studying a particular Bible story, consider acting it out. Or invite someone to visit the class as a biblical character and let the class have conversation with the character.

Is there artwork available for you to show the class to help draw out feelings and emotions about a particular aspect of a lesson? Are there particular crafts the class could work on either individually or as a group that would illustrate some of the lesson's content?

Don't overlook the fact that people can be an important resource. Look at the skills and talents of the people in your congregation. How could you incorporate these human resources into the curriculum?

Look around your church, your community, and your classroom. You will be surprised at the things you can find that can be used to enable your students to experience the lessons you are teaching and to broaden their understanding of God's love for them.

Your Current Curriculum Resources

Use this form to help you examine the curriculum resources you are currently using.

The resources I am using are

___ Bible-to-life
___ Life-to-Bible

These resources are

___ Dated
___ Undated

The resource components include

___ Teacher book
___ Student book
___ Student activity sheets
___ Take-home leaflets
___ Compact disk
___ Audio cassette
___ Resource packet
___ Video
___ Reproducible pages
___ Other:

____

____

____

____

If you are using a dated resource, briefly describe its overall cycle. If you are uncertain about the cycle, the teacher guide may have a description. (Example: Covers the major themes of the Bible in a three-year cycle following the seasons of the church year.)

If you are using undated resources, what is the plan for how you select what will be used?

List additional curriculum resources beyond the printed resources that you use frequently.

Using Curriculum Resources

Have you ever looked at a set of blueprints? While the blueprints will give you some idea about what the house may look like when it is finished, there is a lot of information that the blueprints do not include. Is the house to be built on a corner lot, in a cul-de-sac, or out in the country? What color schemes will be used throughout the house? Do the floors have carpet, vinyl, or wood on them? One must draw upon many resources in addition to the blueprints in order to make the final product. In addition, blueprints are flexible. Changes can be made to the blueprints before construction is begun to meet specific needs and preferences of the family who will be moving into the house.

Blueprints serve as a guide to the overall design of what the house will look like. They help the builder know what materials to buy and how much. The blueprints for a teacher are the teaching plan you use to teach your class. The teaching plan gives you the overall objective and plan for what you will do when the class gathers. Your teaching plan will help you know what activities you intend to do and what supplies you need for each activity.

The teaching plan will not describe the mood of the students before they arrive, or a tragedy your students may have encountered during the week, or questions the students may ask during class. But a good teaching plan will help you to be flexible and make changes for such circumstances that may arise within the life of the students.

Before You Begin to Plan

When you accept the invitation to teach, there are some things you will need to know about your class. The following are some possible questions you will want to ask:

- What are the ages of the students I will be teaching?
- Are there tables and chairs in the room?
- Does this class prefer discussion, lecture, creative learning experiences, or other methods?
- How large is the class?
- Are ages or grades combined to form a class?
- Does this class have special-interest subjects they wish to study?

- How well do the class members know one another?
- Is this a newly formed class, or has this class been established for a period of time?
- What are the class's expectations for our time together?
- Do some of the students have particular needs related to vision, hearing, or a disability?
- Does my church have an overall purpose and vision for Christian education?
- How does the material given to me support that purpose and vision?
- What other supplies are available to help me teach my class?
- Is the space I have been assigned safe and clean?
- How long will I be teaching?
- Who will support me as I teach—the pastor, parents, the education/nurture committee, a coordinator, friends?
- Is teacher training available?

Planning a Lesson

Use this checklist to help you plan your class time. Start far enough ahead that you have time for your own reflection on the material to be presented.

___ Begin with prayer. Ask God to guide you as you teach. Pray for the students in your class.

___ Read the purpose of the session. Look for a purpose statement or a listing of expected outcomes at the beginning of the teacher material.

___ Review the lesson plan in the leader's guide carefully, taking into consideration the needs of your students and adapting the lesson to fit the needs and circumstances of your class.

___ Plan the room arrangement to awaken interest and invite purposeful activity.

___ Outline your plan for the session, giving attention to students' arrival, meeting/together time, dismissal, and at-home experiences related to the session.

___ Plan activities that will involve the students. If you are team teaching, decide who will lead which activities.

___ Try all activities yourself to see if they work.

___ Assemble needed supplies.

As You Teach

Be prepared

- for the students to not like what you have planned
- to alter your plans to fit the needs of the session
- to take more or less time than what you had planned

Evaluate

After each class, discuss the following questions with your teaching team:

- What went well?
- What changes do we want to make for the next session?
- Are there things that we need to review in the next session?
- Were the purposes of the lesson fulfilled?

Adapting Curriculum Resources

Sometimes teachers assume that they should follow the suggested lesson plan exactly and never adapt or deviate from it. This usually leads to frustration and disappointment. Remember that curriculum resources are designed for a wide general audience. You know the students in your class better than any curriculum writer ever will. You know the limits and possibilities created by your facilities, your supplies, your class size, and the abilities of your students.

Whether you will be using dated or undated curriculum resources, you will have to adapt the material to some degree for the age level of your class, the teaching setting, and your style of teaching. Adapting means adjusting the curriculum so that it fits the needs of your students and the environment in which you will be teaching.

Even the best lesson needs to be adapted for each particular group. If an activity doesn't seem to be working for you, consider substituting another one. Be flexible in your planning, and remember that people learn in different ways.

Most curriculum resources suggest more learning activities and approaches than you can possibly fit into your classroom time. You will need to make choices. As you adapt and choose learning experiences, keep in mind the purpose of your lesson. You may think of a learning experience that will accomplish the purpose better with your class than anything suggested in your teacher guide.

Occasionally something will occur in the classroom that is so significant that you may need to throw out your entire lesson plan and deal with the issue at hand.

Adapting the material to fit the needs of those in your class takes time and thought, but it is well worth the effort.

About Learning

As you use your curriculum resources, it is helpful to consider the variety of ways in which your students learn, such as by

- doing
- hearing
- seeing
- repetition
- accident
- failure
- reading
- singing
- teaching
- experimenting
- observing
- discussing
- correction

The Cone of Learning

Edgar Dale, an educational researcher, developed an educational model referred to as the cone of learning. According to Dale, people remember

- 10% of what they read
- 20% of what they hear
- 30% of what they see
- 50% of what they hear and see
- 70% of what they say and write
- 90% of what they say and do

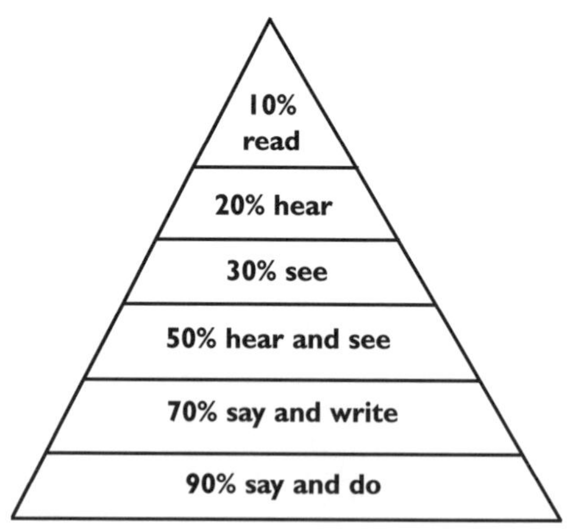

Adapted from *Audio-Visual Methods in Teaching, Third Edition*, by Edgar Dale (Holt, Rinehart, & Winston, Inc., 1969).

If Dale is correct, it is important for teachers to engage students in learning that uses a variety of the senses.

Things to Remember

The well-prepared teacher

- reads the lesson thoroughly
- sees the objective clearly
- knows the pupils intimately
- plans the lessons carefully
- remembers all prayerfully

For Personal Reflection

Look at your lesson plan for the next session you will be teaching. What is the purpose of the lesson? Based on your class, what adaptations do you need to make to the lesson plan? Which learning activities will engage students in saying and doing?

Finding Resources

The curriculum resources that your class uses should be part of your congregation's comprehensive plan for educational ministries. Some churches have an education ministry team or other group that looks at the overall plan for education in the congregation and chooses or recommends curriculum. In some churches, and most often in adult classes, the class or the teacher decides which curriculum resources will be used.

Choosing which curriculum resources to use for a specific setting can seem like an overwhelming task. Where do you look? How do you know what to pick? Who can answer questions about the resources? Fortunately, there is help available. In addition to the information in this chapter, the final chapter of this booklet, "Helpful Resources," lists websites and other resources that will help you find curriculum resources.

United Methodist Curriculum Resources

An official United Methodist curriculum resource is a resource that has been evaluated and approved by the Curriculum Resources Committee of The United Methodist Church. These resources are part of a comprehensive plan for curriculum designed to ensure that local congregations have the resources needed to carry out their educational ministries with people of all ages.

Forecast

Forecast is a quarterly catalog that describes curriculum resources for the upcoming quarter and provides an order form. Your pastor and whoever orders the curriculum for your church school setting receive *Forecast* each quarter.

A larger, annual copy of Forecast is also available. The annual edition includes a wide variety of curriculum resources for all age groups.

Resources that are approved United Methodist resources are designated in *Forecast* with the CRC logo.

The Curriculum Resources Committee of The United Methodist General Board of Discipleship has approved this resource for use in the Christian education ministry of The United Methodist Church.

Curric-U-Phone

Curric-U-Phone is a toll-free number (800-251-8591) that can link you with a curriculum consultant at The United Methodist Publishing House. The Curric-U-Phone consultants can answer questions about current United Methodist curriculum resources, suggest appropriate resources for your setting, and help you plan what curriculum resources you would like to use in the future. You can also contact Curric-U-Phone by e-mail at curricuphone@cokesbury.com.

Cokesbury Action Teams

Cokesbury Action Teams are available in some areas to consult, counsel, and lead workshops in local churches. Call Curric-U-Phone at 800-251-8591 for more information.

Cokesbury Stores

Cokesbury stores are found in locations throughout the United States. United Methodist curriculum resources are available at Cokesbury stores. Here you can also find a wide range of supplemental material to support the curriculum you are using.

Conference and District Offices

Your annual conference staff and district superintendent receive a limited display of sample age-level curriculum on a quarterly basis. Many conferences have staff who can assist local churches with teacher training or curriculum consultation. Write or call your conference office. Check with your pastor to find out whom you need to contact at the conference office.

For Personal Reflection

How is the curriculum for your class selected? Look through a copy of *Forecast* and make note of curriculum resources that might be helpful for your class. If you do not have a copy of *Forecast*, you can request one by calling Curric-U-Phone.

The Most Important Curriculum

As you have read through this booklet and have begun to think about what you will be teaching, the supplies you will need in the classroom, and the interest of your students, don't forget about the most important curriculum in the classroom: YOU, the teacher. Some recent surveys have indicated that the teacher is seven times more important than the printed curriculum resources.

Think about a class you participated in as a youth or child. Do you remember the name of the curriculum resources? Do you remember the name of your teacher? Most of us remember the attitudes and values of our teachers long after we have forgotten the lessons that they taught.

Take the time to adequately prepare your lessons. When you are well prepared, you give the message to the members of your class that you value your time together and believe that what happens in class is important.

Preparing to teach involves more than having a lesson plan and gathering supplies. You also prepare to teach as you nurture your relationship with God. Spend time in prayer, in Bible study, and in worship. It is difficult to help others become disciples if you are not a disciple yourself.

Use the assessment on pages 39 and 40 to evaluate where you are as a teacher and where you need to grow.

Assessing My Needs for Growing as a Teacher/Leader

In each category, write yes beside the things you are doing, no beside the things you are not doing. Indicate whether each item is something you can do on your own, or whether you need support through training, other people, or information.

Spiritual Life

____ Reading the Bible
____ Keeping a journal
____ Praying
____ Attending worship
____ Other things I do or would like to do:

____

____

____

Planning

____ Understanding how to use the material
____ Adapting the material to fit my class
____ Locating supplies
____ Planning activities to fit the needs of the class
____ Praying for my class
____ Other things I do or would like to do:

____

____

____

Teacher Enrichment

____ Attending teacher training
____ Meeting with other teachers
____ Sharing ideas about lessons I will be teaching
____ Other things I do or would like to do:

____

____

____

Classroom Teaching

____ Setting up the classroom
____ Understanding the group I teach
____ Trying new ideas
____ Working as a member of a teaching team
____ Preparing for mission
____ Helping the class members be in ministry
____ Other things I do or would like to do:

____

____

____

Recordkeeping

____ Following up on absentees
____ Sending birthday greetings
____ Following up on visitors
____ Other things I do or would like to do:

____

____

____

Going Further

As you prepare your lessons and teach your class, remember that you are not expected to make a Christian of every person you teach. You are expected to provide opportunities that open the Scriptures, excite curiosity, support thoughtful inquiry, and assist in important decisions being made about the Christian faith journey.

As you engage in this task you will find yourself evaluating the curriculum resources you are using. The criteria you use to evaluate your curriculum will depend upon what you hope will be accomplished in your class. The following questions provide a helpful starting place for developing curriculum criteria.

- Do the resources fit the needs of the class?
- Do the resources fit with the overall purpose of the Christian education program of our church?

- Is the curriculum helping us grow as faithful disciples of Jesus Christ?
- How are different cultures and races depicted?
- Are people with disabilities depicted in the resources?
- What does the curriculum imply or say directly about the nature of God?
- How is the Bible used?
- Does the curriculum encourage class members to take action related to what they are learning?
- Are the beliefs expressed in the resources consistent with our church's beliefs?
- What learning styles are used in the curriculum?
- What additional materials are needed to successfully use these resources?
- What space is needed to effectively use these resources?
- How does the teacher's guide help me grow in faith, knowledge, and skills?

For Personal Reflection

Make a list of the most important criteria for evaluating curriculum for your class. Using the list, evaluate the curriculum resources you are currently using.

Helpful Resources

Websites

General Board of Discipleship of The United Methodist Church (www.gbod.org). On this site you will find articles related to discipleship and teaching. You will also find a list of the Christian Education Staff available to consult, counsel, and assist with curriculum ideas and selection. Other sites of particular interest are www.gbod.org/education and www.gbod.org/keepingintouch.

Discipleship Resources (www.discipleshipresources.org). In this online bookstore you can purchase additional copies of this booklet, other booklets in the series, and other books published by Discipleship Resources, such as other teacher resources and books that can be used in small-group settings.

Cokesbury (www.cokesbury.com). This site offers information on United Methodist curriculum for all ages.

Cokesbury Training (www.ilearntoteach.com). This Cokesbury site offers teacher training opportunities.

The Upper Room (www.upperroom.org). On this website you will find resources for spiritual formation in small groups.

Books

Keeping in Touch: Christian Formation and Teaching, by Carol F. Krau (Discipleship Resources, 1999). Provides an overview of five processes important for teachers as they seek to help people grow as disciples.

Out of the Basement: A Holistic Approach to Children's Ministry, by Diane C. Olson (Discipleship Resources, 2001). Includes criteria for evaluating children's curriculum.

Start Here: Teaching and Learning With Adults, by Barbara Bruce (Discipleship Resources, 2000). Basic book for teachers of adults. Includes lesson planning, adult faith development, and learning styles.

Ordering Information

Resources published by Discipleship Resources may be ordered online at www.discipleshipresources.org; by phone at 800-685-4370; by fax at 770-442-9742; or by mail from Discipleship Resources Distribution Center, P.O. Box 1616, Alpharetta, GA 30009-1616.